Dolphins

Dolphins

Dean Stahl

THE CHILD'S WORLD®, INC.

Published in the United States of America by The Child's World®, Inc.
PO Box 326
Chanhassen, MN 55317-0326
800-599-READ
www.childsworld.com

Product Manager Mary Berendes
Editor Katherine Stevenson
Designer Mary Berendes
Contributor Bob Temple

Photo Credits
© Alejandro Robles/Marine Mammal Images: 10
© 2001 Brandon D. Cole: 2, 6, 13, 23
© Daniel J. Cox/naturalexposures.com: 9, 19
© François Gohier: cover, 24
© Gregory Ochocki/Marine Mammal Images: 15
© Ingrid Visser/Ursus Photography: 29
© Jasmine Rossi: 16
© Jeffrey L. Rotman: 20, 26
© 2001 Stuart Westmorland/Stone: 30

Library of Congress Cataloging-in-Publication Data
Stahl, Dean.
Dolphins / by Dean Stahl.
p. cm.
Includes index.
ISBN 1-56766-889-5 (library bound : alk. paper)
1. Dolphins—Juvenile literature. [1. Dolphins.] I. Title.
QL737.C432 S63 2001
599.53—dc21
00-010774

On the cover...

Front cover: This bottlenose dolphin is curious about the photographer.
Page 2: These Atlantic spotted dolphins are swimming together in the open ocean.

Table of Contents

A ship is sailing on the ocean under a clear blue sky. In front of the ship, fishlike animals keep appearing and disappearing in the waves. These sleek animals leap clear of the water and then dive back in. They have no trouble keeping up with the speeding ship. What are these speedy animals? They're dolphins!

⇐ This Pacific white-sided dolphin is playing in front of a ship.

What Are Dolphins?

Unlike other ocean creatures, dolphins and whales belong to a group of animals called **mammals.** Mammals breathe air and have warm blood in their bodies. They also feed their babies milk that they make in their bodies. Cows and people are mammals, too.

Dolphins are different from most other whales because they have teeth—lots of teeth! Most whales simply open their huge mouths and swallow their meals whole. Dolphins, however, use their pointed teeth to catch and tear up their food. They have anywhere from 88 to 200 teeth—more than any other mammal.

Here you can see this bottlenose dolphin's teeth. ⇒

Dolphins are sometimes confused with *porpoises,* another water mammal. Porpoises and dolphins, however, are two different animals. Most porpoises are smaller than dolphins. They also have a shorter snout. One of the biggest differences between porpoises and dolphins is their teeth. Porpoises have flatter, spade-shaped teeth. Dolphins' teeth are cone-shaped.

⇐ Gulf of California harbor porpoises (or vaquitas) like this one are very rare. Scientists think there are fewer than five hundred of these animals alive today.

What Do Dolphins Look Like?

A dolphin's sleek body is shaped to slip easily through the water. The dolphin's skin is so smooth, it feels just like an inner tube! This slick skin lets the dolphin glide through water as easily as you can zoom down a slide.

A **dorsal fin** in the middle of the dolphin's back helps keep the dolphin stable as it swims. To move forward, the dolphin uses its powerful tail to push through the water. To change directions, the dolphin steers with its front flippers.

These Atlantic spotted dolphins are swimming ⇒
off the coast of Grand Bahama Island.

Are There Different Kinds of Dolphins?

There are more than 31 different kinds, or **species,** of dolphins. Most dolphins live in the salty waters of the world's oceans. Some dolphins, such as the *Atlantic white-sided dolphin* and the *hourglass dolphin,* live in colder parts of the world. Others, such as the *bottlenose dolphin,* live in warmer waters. Bottlenose dolphins are one of the most famous dolphin species. People often see them in zoos and aquariums.

A few dolphin species live in freshwater. These animals live in warm, tropical rivers such as the Amazon. The *Ganges dolphin* and the *Amazon River dolphin* are two types that live in freshwater.

Amazon River dolphins like this one have very long snouts. ⇒

Another kind of saltwater dolphin is the "killer whale," or *orca*. Orcas are the biggest members of the dolphin family. Some orcas can grow to be over 30 feet long. That's as long as two small cars!

Orcas eat bigger ocean foods such as seals and large fish. Sometimes orcas even eat other dolphins. Orcas can be dangerous, but some have been taught to live in zoos and water parks. These orcas are friendly to people and can even perform tricks.

⇐ This orca is swimming up onto a Patagonian beach on purpose. It is looking for seals to eat.

How Do Dolphins Breathe?

Like all mammals, dolphins breathe with their lungs. The top of a dolphin's head has a hole that can open and shut very quickly. It is called a **blowhole.** When the blowhole is open, air flows to the dolphin's lungs. When the dolphin goes underwater, the blowhole shuts. Dolphins breathe about once every two minutes. Sometimes they dive deep underwater to catch fish. They can hold their breath for over seven minutes!

You can see the blowholes on these two dolphins, ⇒ which are resting in a Honduras zoo.

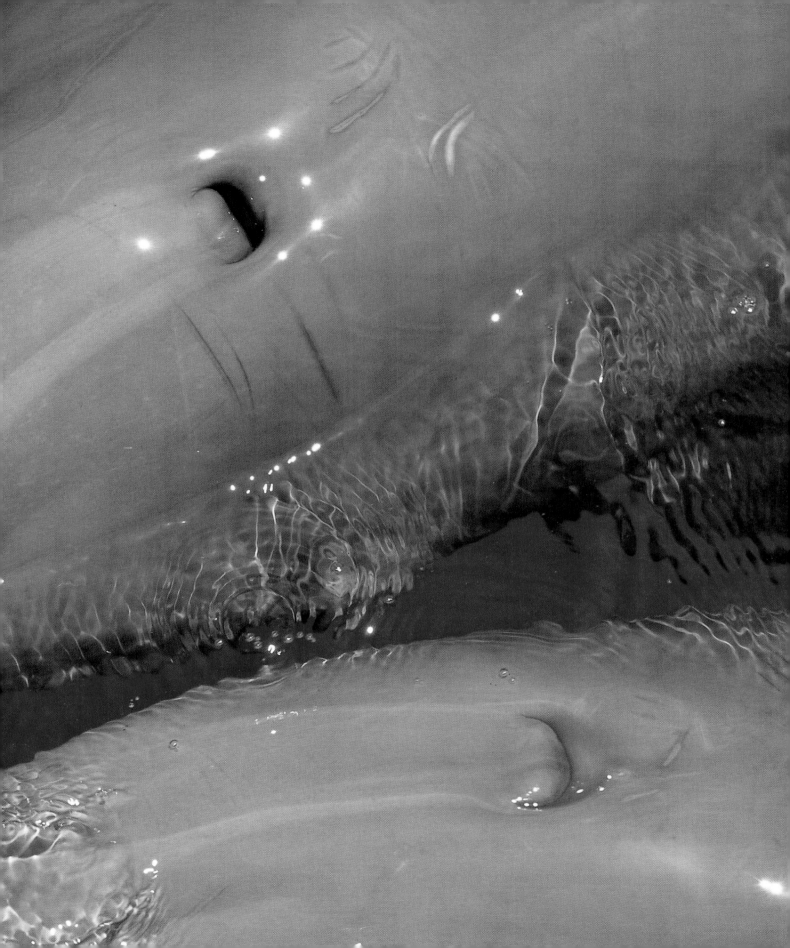

Dolphins are **carnivores,** which means that they eat other animals. Dolphins love to eat small fish, squid, and sometimes little jellyfish. What a dolphin eats depends on where it lives. Dolphin species that live in colder areas eat fish such as salmon and herring. Dolphins in warmer areas love to snack on shrimp and eels.

⇐ This wild bottlenose dolphin has found an octopus to eat.

How Do Dolphins Find Their Food?

The ocean is deep and dark. So how does a dolphin find its fast-swimming dinner? Most dolphins have very good eyesight. But their hearing is even better—especially when it comes to finding dinner! Dolphins make squeaking and clicking noises underwater. The noises bounce off whatever is nearby, including fish. When the sound bounces back, the dolphin can tell exactly where the fish is swimming. This way of finding things is called **echolocation**—the dolphins "locate" things by listening to the "echoes" of the clicks.

These Pacific white-sided dolphins are using ⇒ echolocation to find food in dark ocean waters.

How Do Dolphins Communicate?

Dolphins use their bodies to communicate with other dolphins. They smack the water with their tails and flippers. They snap their jaws. When they are really excited, some dolphins even leap out of the water.

Dolphins also whistle, click, and squeak by moving air inside their throats and heads. Sometimes they make sounds with their blowholes. Some dolphin noises sound like a creaking door. Others sound like laughter! Dolphins use these sounds to "talk" to other dolphins and even to warn them of danger. Scientists have been studying dolphins for many years to learn whether they have a language. They still aren't sure about a dolphin "language." But they do think that each dolphin uses a special whistle to identify itself.

⇐ These wild bottlenose dolphins are playing together. They must swim very fast to get enough speed to jump out of the water.

What Are Baby Dolphins Like?

Like all mammals, dolphins give birth to live young. Usually, a dolphin mother has only one baby, or **calf,** at a time. The calf weighs about 10 pounds when it is born. It can swim right away—but not very well. In fact, other dolphins must help the newborn to the surface so it can take its first breath.

For the first year or so, the calf stays very close to its mother. At first, it drinks the milk its mother makes in her body. The milk is very thick (a little like cottage cheese) and helps the baby grow up strong. Over time, the calf learns how to hunt fish on its own.

⇐ This bottlenose dolphin calf and its mother are swimming in the Red Sea near Egypt.

Are Dolphins in Danger?

Dolphins protect themselves by swimming in groups called **pods.** Many pods are small, but some have as many as 2,500 dolphins. Dolphins that stray from their pod are sometimes hunted by hungry orcas or sharks. But people and the pollution we cause are a bigger threat.

Another danger is fishing nets. Fishing boats follow dolphin pods to find fish, such as tuna, that often swim below the pods. When the boats put out nets to catch the tuna, the nets sometimes hurt or kill dolphins. Many people are working hard to keep these accidents from happening. Even so, tuna nets are still a danger to dolphins.

This pod of dusky dolphins is swimming in the open ocean. ⇒

Dolphins are some of the smartest animals on Earth. They are able to solve problems and can learn how to do tricks or even save people's lives. Scientists have been studying dolphins for many years to discover more about these fascinating animals. As we keep exploring the oceans, we'll learn more about dolphins and how they live.

⇐ This bottlenose dolphin in Honduras is curious about the photographer.

Glossary

blowhole (BLOH-hole)
A dolphin's blowhole is the opening at the top of the dolphin's head.
Dolphins use their blowholes for breathing and sometimes for
making sounds.

calf (KAF)
A baby dolphin is called a calf. A dolphin calf can swim as soon as it
is born.

carnivores (KAR-nih-vorz)
Carnivores are animals that eat other animals. Dolphins are carnivores.

dorsal fin (DOR-sull FIN)
A dolphin's dorsal fin is the fin on its back. The dorsal fin helps keep
the dolphin steady in the water as it swims.

echolocation (eh-koh-loh-KAY-shun)
Echolocation is the way dolphins find things in dark waters.
Dolphins find things they can't see by making clicking sounds and
listening to the echoes.

mammals (MAM-ullz)
Mammals are animals that have warm blood and produce milk for
their babies. Dolphins are mammals, even though they look like fish.

pods (PODZ)
Dolphins travel in groups called pods. Fishing boats follow dolphin
pods to find other kinds of fish that swim nearby.

species (SPEE-sheez)
A species is a different kind of an animal. There are more than 31
different species of dolphin.

Web Sites

http://www.cetacea.org/dolphins.htm

http://oceanlink.island.net/aquafacts/dolphin.html

http://www.dolphinresearch.org.au/index.html

http://library.thinkquest.org/17963/index-1.shtml

Index